NATIONAL GEOGRAPHIC
KIDS

weird
but
true!

300 outrageous facts

NATIONAL GEOGRAPHIC

VISIT US ONLINE:
Kids: nationalgeographic.com/kids
Parents: nationalgeographic.com
Teachers: nationalgeographic.com/education
Librarians: ngchildrensbooks.org

For information about special discounts for bulk
purchases, please contact National Geographic Books
Special Sales: ngspecsales@ngs.org

For rights or permissions inquiries, please contact
National Geographic Books Subsidiary Rights:
ngbookrights@ngs.org

Library of Congress Cataloging-in-Publication Data
Weird but true: 300 outrageous facts.
     p. cm.
Includes index.
ISBN 978-1-4263-0594-8 (pbk. : alk. paper)
1. Curiosities and wonders--Juvenile literature.
I. National Geographic Society (U.S.)
AG243.W39 2010 001.9--dc22
2009028459
Scholastic edition ISBN 978-1-4263-0723-2

Printed in China
09/RRDS/1

Cheetahs
can change
direction in
midair when
chasing
prey.

A SHEEP, A DUCK, AND A ROOSTER WERE THE FIRST PASSENGERS ON A HOT-AIR BALLOON.

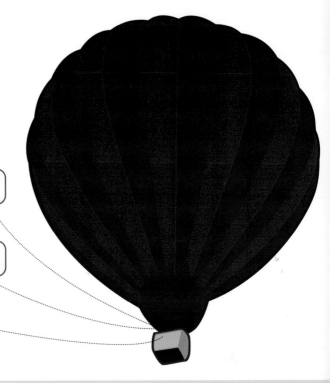

Google.com is named after the number googol—

10000000000000000000
00000000000000000000
00000000000000000000

Tia the Neapolitan **mastiff** gave birth to **24 puppies** in one litter.

Girls have more taste buds than **boys** do.

a one followed by a hundred zeros.

OOOOOOOOOOOOOOOOOOOOOOOO
OOOOOOOOOOOOOOOOOOOOOOOOOO
OOOOOOOOOOOOOOOOOOOOOOO

The
tallest
known
snowman
was
higher than
a 12-story
building.

8

SOME
HONEYBEE
QUEENS
QUACK.

A bat can eat **3,000** **insects** in one **night.**

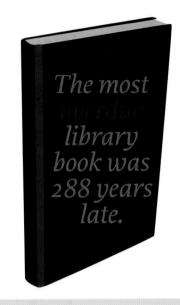

The most overdue library book was 288 years late.

The **largest working** **yo-yo** was more than 10 feet (3 m) tall and weighed almost 900 pounds (408 kg) —as much as a **polar bear.**

Star Wars creators designed Yoda to look like Albert Einstein.

IN JAPAN, IT'S POSSIBLE TO BUY WATERMELONS SHAPED LIKE PYRAMIDS.

167 letters

Krungthep
Ratanakosin Mahinthar
Mahadilokpop Nopar
Udomratchanivet Maha
Avatarnsathit Sakkath
officially known as

are in the world's longest place-name, Mahanakhon Bovorn ayutthaya atratchathani Burirom sathan Amornpiman attiyavisnukarmprasit, **Bangkok, Thailand.**

New York City's Empire State Building was built with ten million bricks.

A coffin was once designed to look like a lobster.

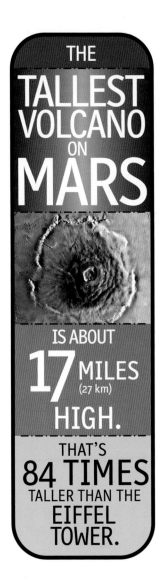

THE **TALLEST VOLCANO** ON **MARS**

IS ABOUT **17** MILES (27 km) **HIGH.**

THAT'S **84 TIMES** TALLER THAN THE **EIFFEL TOWER.**

PEANUT
BUTTER
CAN BE
CONVERTED INTO A
DIAMOND.

If you could travel the speed of light, you would never get older.

BELLY BUTTON LINT

IS MADE OF CLOTHING FIBERS, HAIR, AND DEAD SKIN CELLS.

THE OLDEST CONTINUOUSLY STANDING TREE ON EARTH IS NEARLY 5,000 YEARS OLD— ABOUT THE SAME AGE AS THE PYRAMIDS OF EGYPT.

A woman hand-delivered a pizza from London, England, to Melbourne, Australia— a distance of about **10,350 miles.**

(16,657 km)

Your **FINGERNAILS** take six months to grow from base to tip.

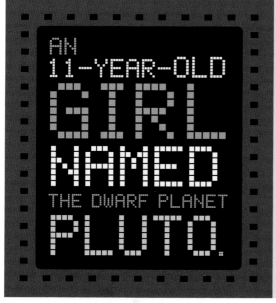

AN 11-YEAR-OLD **GIRL NAMED** THE DWARF PLANET **PLUTO.**

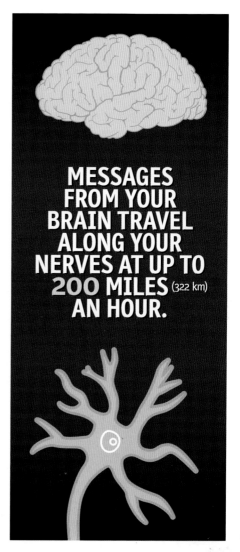

MESSAGES FROM YOUR BRAIN TRAVEL ALONG YOUR NERVES AT UP TO 200 MILES (322 km) **AN HOUR.**

A SNEEZE TRAVELS 100 MILES AN HOUR.

(161 km)

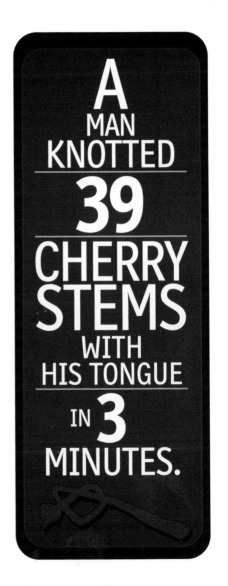

A MAN KNOTTED 39 CHERRY STEMS WITH HIS TONGUE IN 3 MINUTES.

The world's **biggest flower**—found in the Indonesian rain forest—can grow **wider than a car tire.**

THE FOUNDERS OF THE

TOY COMPANY

DOLLS AFTER THEIR

KEN AND

BARB

MATTEL NAMED TWO CHILDREN:

IE.

THERE ARE ABOUT A BILLION BACTERIA IN YOUR MOUTH RIGHT NOW.

Cockroaches can survive underwater for up to 15 minutes.

The first bubble gum, made in 1906, was called Blibber-Blubber.

ABOUT TEN THOUSAND OF THE CELLS IN YOUR BODY COULD FIT ON THE HEAD OF A PIN.

Applesauce was the first food eaten in space by an American astronaut.

Phasmophobia is the fear of ghosts.

A blue whale's **heart** weighs up to 2,000 pounds.
(907 kg)

Slugs have 3,000 teeth

and 4 noses.

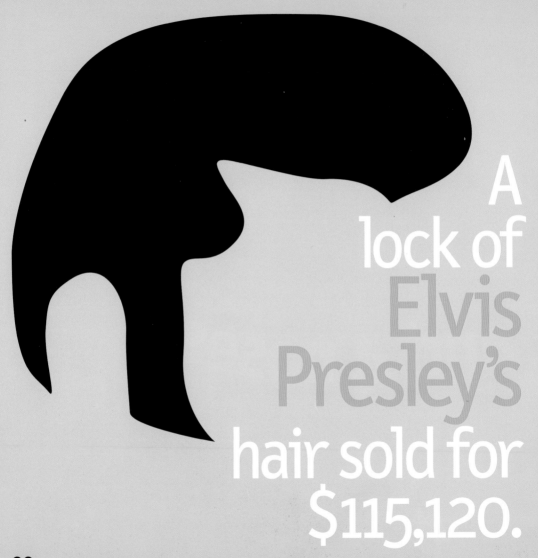

A lock of Elvis Presley's hair sold for $115,120.

SOME CARS
CAN RUN ON
USED FRENCH-
FRY OIL.

HOT DOGS
CAN LAST MORE THAN 20 YEARS
IN LANDFILLS.

The eastern spotted **skunk** does *a handstand* before it **sprays.**

About a million Earths could fit inside the **sun.**

THE BRIGHTEST LIGHT ON A HOTEL—IN LAS VEGAS, NEVADA, IN THE UNITED STATES— CAN BE SEEN FROM AIRPLANES 250 MILES AWAY. (402 km)

THE PROTOTYPE OF THE ORIGINAL G.I. JOE DOLL SOLD FOR $200,000.

Almost **90%** of **snow** is **air.**

HONEY
NEVER
SPOILS.

THE WORLD'S LIGHTEST MAMMAL —THE BUMBLEBEE BAT— **WEIGHS** ABOUT AS MUCH AS TWO M&M'S.

MOTHS CAN SMELL EACH OTHER FROM MILES AWAY.

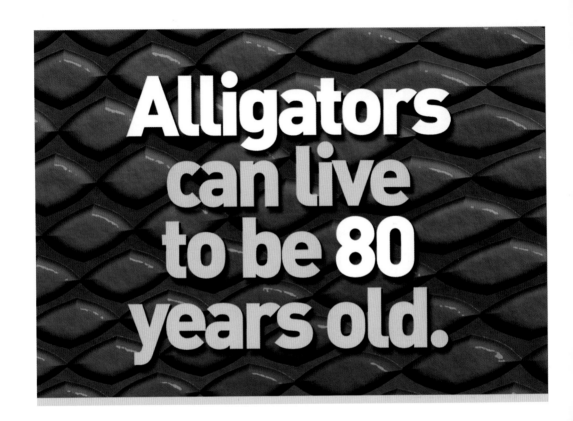

Alligators can live to be 80 years old.

A large python can swall

Bats
are the only mammals that fly.

SOME SNAILS CAN SLEEP FOR THREE YEARS.

OW a goat whole.

41

SOME FROGS CAN GLIDE UP TO 50 FEET (15 m) THROUGH THE AIR.

A camel doesn't **sweat** until its body temperature reaches **106°F.** (41°c)

Writers once used **bread crumbs** instead of erasers to correct pencil mistakes.

A waterfall in Hawaii sometimes goes up instead of down.

Cats

communicate using at least 16 known "cat words."

A beefalo is part bison, part cow.

A man **sculpted a statue** of himself using his own **hair, teeth, and nails.**

IF GRASSHOPPERS WERE THE SIZE OF PEOPLE, THEY COULD LEAP THE LENGTH OF A BASKETBALL COURT.

BOLTS OF LIGHTNING CAN SHOOT OUT OF AN ERUPTING VOLCANO.

HORSES RUN ON THEIR toes.

Dragonflies can see in all directions at once.

There are
29
different
shades of
red Crayola
crayons.

brick red

magenta

red

violet red

red violet

wild strawb

IT'S POSSIBLE FOR A SHARK TO DETECT A **FISH'S HEARTBEAT** BEFORE IT ATTACKS.

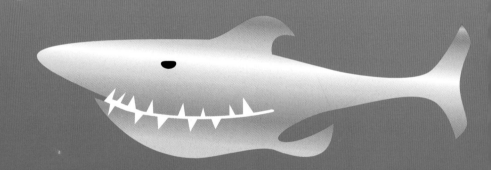

You can buy a piece of meteorite on eBay.

THE **clock** ON THE **hundred-dollar bill** SAYS **4:10.**

WEDDING GOWNS HAVE BEEN MADE OUT OF TOILET PAPER.

SOME **FISH** CAN WALK ON LAND.

You can see a **1,700-pound** (771 kg) chocolate **moose** named **Lenny** in Maine, in the U.S.A.

Scuba divers send postcards from a mailbox off the coast of **japan** that's nearly **33 feet** (10 m) **underwater.**

The **LARGEST pumpkin pie** WEIGHED **2,020 pounds** (916 kg).

53

DOLPHINS CAN HEAR SOUNDS UNDERWATER FROM 15 MILES (24 km) AWAY.

African elephants have ears shaped like the continent of Africa.

Porcupines CAN float.

An average yawn lasts about six seconds.

Koalas and **humans** have similar fingerprints.

Opposite sides of **dice** always add up to **7.**

IT'S ILLEGAL TO SELL A **HAUNTED HOUSE** IN NEW YORK **WITHOUT TELLING** THE BUYER.

Some elephant seals dive DEEPER than most submarines.

It gets so cold in **Siberia** that your breath can turn to ice in midair.

A BRITISH WEBSITE SELLS LAND ON
MARS...

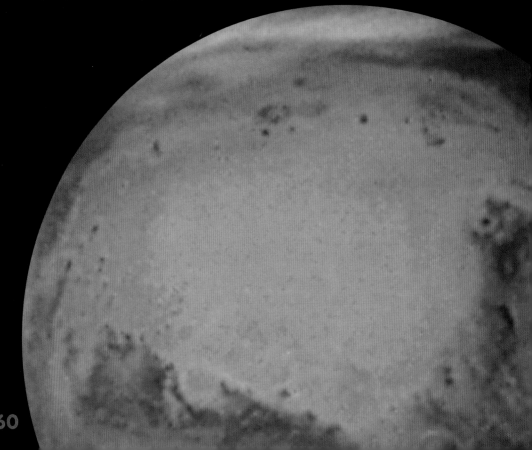

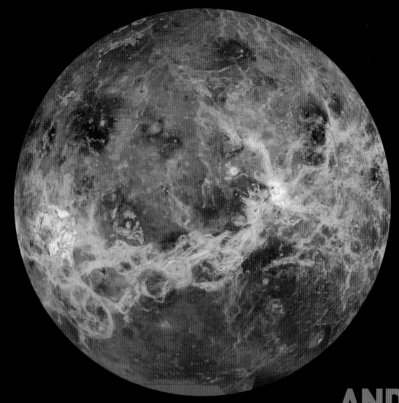

AND
VENUS
FOR £16.75
(ABOUT $29) AN ACRE.

61

A male ostrich can

roar

like a
LION.

Hippo sweat is
red.

Some salamanders regrow their tails, legs, and even parts of their eyes.

A tiger's skin is

like its fur.

A ZEDONK

IS A CROSS BETWEEN A FEMALE DONKEY AND A MALE ZEBRA.

Abracadabra

used to be written in a triangle shape to keep away evil spirits.

ABRACADABRA
ABRACADABR
ABRACADAB
ABRACADA
ABRACAD
ABRACA
ABRAC
ABRA
ABR
AB
A

A **Slinky** can **stretch** from a sixth-floor window to the ground.

SOME ANTS MAKE THEMSELVES EXPLODE WHEN ATTACKED.

Chameleons change color in as fast as 20 seconds.

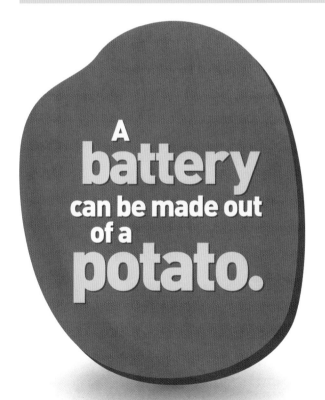

A **battery** can be made out of a **potato.**

JELLYFISH STING EVEN WHEN DEAD.

Your eyes move about 80 times a second.

A lobster's teeth are in its stomach.

A DOLPHIN CAN LEARN TO RECOGNIZE ITSELF IN THE MIRROR.

YOU CAN SEE AUTUMN LEAVES FROM SPACE.

There's a
**heart-
shaped
coral
reef**
in Australia.

At least **12** rocks from **Mars** have landed on **Earth.**

A SLOTH WOULD TAKE A MONTH TO TRAVEL A SINGLE MILE.

A **U.S. dollar bill** can be folded in the same spot about **4,000 times** before it tears.

Chicks can **breathe** through their **shells.**

Pet hamsters **run** up to **eight** miles (13 km) **a night** on a **wheel.**

MORE THAN **60,000 PEOPLE** ARE **FLYING OVER** THE **UNITED STATES** IN AIRPLANES RIGHT NOW.

New York

drifts about an inch (2.5 cm) farther from

London

every year.

In the open ocean, a **tsunami** sometimes travels as fast as a jet plane.

A mountain climber carried the **Olympic torch** to the top of **Mount Everest.**

Owls can't move their eyeballs.

From **Earth** you always look at the **same side** of the **moon.**

THE BIGGEST BALD EAGLE NESTS WEIGH UP TO 4,000 POUNDS. (1,814 kg)

Kangaroos don't hop backward.

It's possible for people to get **goosebumps** on their faces.

Some **humming-birds** weigh less than a **penny.**

Tornadoes usually spin in opposite directions above and below the Equator.

It would take about three years of nonstop pedaling to bike to the moon.

Food passes through the **giant squid's** brain on the way to its **stomach.**

Clams can live to be more than a hundred years old.

WHO ARE YOU CALLING OLD?

The end of the minute hand on **London's Big Ben** clock travels about **118** miles (190 km) a year.

In a lifetime, the average American drives approximately

627,000 miles (1,009,059 km)

or 25 times around the world— using enough gasoline to fill 3 fuel tankers.

An avalanche can travel **80** MILES (129 km) AN HOUR.

A church IN THE Czech Republic HAS A chandelier made of human bones.

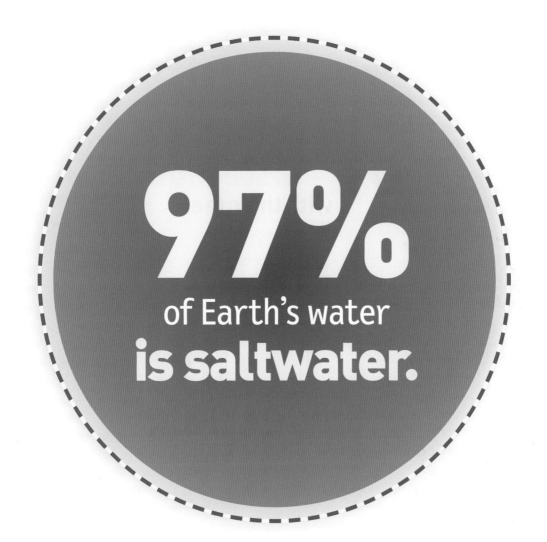

97%
of Earth's water
is saltwater.

Dust from Africa can travel all the way to Florida.

Humans can recognize about **10,000** different smells.

BUTTERFLIES taste food with their feet.

A BASEBALL WILL TRAVEL FARTHER IN **HOT** WEATHER THAN IN **COLD** WEATHER.

Snakes can't slither on glass.

A RESTAURANT OWNER MADE A **6,000-GALLON** (22,706 L) MILKSHAKE—ENOUGH TO FILL MORE THAN **100** BATHTUBS.

HIPPOS
can be
more
dangerous
than
LIONS.

The fastest **falcon** can **outpace** a speeding **race car.**

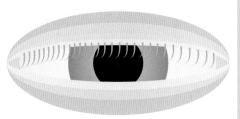

Kids BLINK about **five million** times a year.

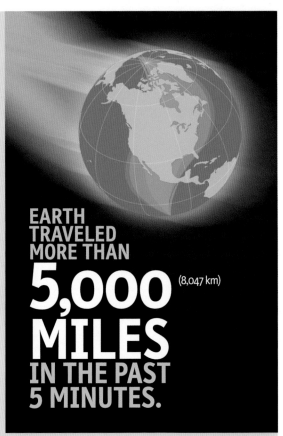

EARTH TRAVELED MORE THAN **5,000** (8,047 km) **MILES** IN THE PAST 5 MINUTES.

(2,710 m)
Bakers in Turkey made an 8,891-foot-long cake— that's the length of about 114 tennis courts!

The Himalayan **mountains** grow a half inch taller each year.

IF ABOUT
33 MILLION
PEOPLE
HELD HANDS,
THEY COULD MAKE
A CIRCLE AROUND
THE EQUATOR.

An ant can carry

50 TIMES

its body weight.

(That's like a kid carrying a car!)

In ancient Egypt, **mummies' brains** were removed through the **nose.**

THE AVERAGE **$100** BILL CIRCULATES FOR **9** YEARS.

FOUR-THOUSAND-YEAR-OLD NOODLES WERE DISCOVERED IN ANCIENT RUINS IN CHINA.

A HUNDRED-YEAR-OLD CHOCOLATE BAR SOLD FOR NEARLY $700.

THE MOST EXPENSIVE ITEM EVER SOLD ON eBay WAS A $168-MILLION YACHT.

The planet **VENUS** spins backward.

IF YOU HEAT A DIAMOND TO 1405°F, (763°C) IT WILL TURN INTO VAPOR.

PEOPLE REPORT
THE
MOST
UFO
SIGHTINGS
WHEN VENUS
IS CLOSEST
TO EARTH.

Australia was once a British prison colony.

The Asian vampire moth sometimes drinks the blood of animals.

A New York man did a continuous series of somersaults for 12 miles, 390 yards.
(357 m)

A person once **"hiccuped"** for **68** years.

A clock runs faster on a tall mountain than at sea level.

Astronauts orbiting Earth see up to 16 sunrises and sunsets every day.

Many birds' **feathers** weigh more than their **bones.**

A caterpillar

has **more muscles** than a **human.**

You can fry an egg on a hot sidewalk

ICELAND DOESN'T ONLY HAVE EARTHQUAKES; IT ALSO HAS ICEQUAKES.

when it reaches 158°F. (70°C)

Chewing gum burns about **11** calories an hour.

YOUR EYES PROCESS MORE THAN **120** MILLION BITS OF INFORMATION EVERY SECOND.

weighs more than

COLD water

HOT water.

A flea can jump 100 times its body length—that's like you jumping to the top of a 34-story building!

The color red doesn't really make **bulls angry;** they are **color-blind.**

No one knows what color dinosaurs were.

DAYS ARE LONGER THAN YEARS ON THE PLANET MERCURY.

THE FIRST CANDY CANES WERE MADE WITHOUT STRIPES.

Cat urine can glow under black light.

SOME FISH CHANGE FROM FEMALE TO MALE.

The average American eats enough **hamburger meat** in a lifetime to **equal the weight** of a family car.

IF EARTH DIDN'T TILT, WE WOULDN'T HAVE SEASONS.

OUR PLANET HAS THE SAME AMOUNT OF **WATER TODAY** AS IT DID **100 MILLION YEARS AGO.**

A sea turtle
can weigh as much as a
water buffalo.

There are more
PLASTIC

FLAMINGOS
IN THE U.S.A.
than
real ones.

VISION USES
ONE-THIRD OF ALL YOUR BRAINPOWER.

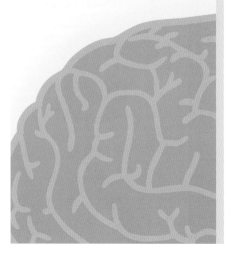

PARACHUTES WERE INVENTED BEFORE AIRPLANES.

An electric eel produces a charge strong enough to

stun a horse.

Spiders have clear blood.

SOME RATS CAN SURVIVE WITHOUT WATER LONGER THAN CAMELS.

MORE PEOPLE LIVE IN CHINA TODAY THAN LIVED ON EARTH 150 YEARS AGO.

Ancient Egyptians believed that a person's **soul** was located in the **heart.**

Olympic gold medals are actually more than 90 percent silver.

The biggest gingerbread house was decorated with **4,750** pounds (2,155 kg) of icing—that's heavier than a **giraffe.**

IS THERE A RECORD FOR THE CUTEST HOUSE?

ASTRONAUTS' FOOTPRINTS STAY ON THE MOON FOREVER; THERE'S NO WIND TO BLOW THEM AWAY.

New Zealand HAS MORE sheep THAN people.

Giant TORTOISES KEEP GROWING FOR THEIR WHOLE LIVES.

MORE THAN
10 MILLION
MILLIONAIRES
ARE ALIVE
TODAY.

AN ARTIST USED 100,000 TOOTHPICKS TO BUILD A FOUR-FOOT-LONG (1.2 m) REMOTE-CONTROL BOAT.

EARTHWORMS HAVE **5** HEARTS.

Ladybugs squirt
smelly liquid from their knees when they *get scared.*

IF YOU *RUN* IN THE RAIN, YOU WILL GET ABOUT **50%** WETTER THAN IF YOU STAND STILL.

IN SOME PLACES THERE ARE ABOUT AS MANY **INSECTS** IN ONE SQUARE MILE (2.6 sq km) AS THERE ARE PEOPLE ON THE ENTIRE **PLANET.**

HONEYBEES CAN BE TRAINED TO DETECT EXPLOSIVES.

Traffic lights were invented

before

CARS.

THERE ARE MORE STARS IN THE UNIVERSE THAN GRAINS OF SAND ON EARTH.

THE LONGEST MONOPOLY GAME PLAYED IN A BATHTUB LASTED **99** HOURS.

Blue whales ARE THE **largest animals** THAT EVER **lived—** THEY'RE EVEN BIGGER THAN **dinosaurs!**

CLEOPATRA BECAME THE QUEEN OF EGYPT WHEN SHE WAS ONLY A TEENAGER.

Panda droppings can be made into paper.

The largest **dinosaurs** were vegetarians.

IT WOULD TAKE **A JUMBO JET** ABOUT **120 BILLION YEARS** TO FLY ACROSS THE MILKY WAY GALAXY.

A **pet** goldfish in England lived to be **43** years old.

RED RAIN HAS FALLEN IN PARTS OF EUROPE AND ASIA.

Catnip can affect lions and tigers.

A 300-YEAR-OLD HURRICANE ON JUPITER IS STILL GOING STRONG!

THE WORLD'S HEAVIEST ONION WEIGHED MORE THAN A MAN'S HEAD.

In **Peru** it's considered **good luck** to wear yellow **underwear** on New Year's **Day.**

SKIN IS YOUR BODY'S LARGEST ORGAN.

THE ANCIENT EGYPTIANS TRAINED MONKEYS TO DANCE AND PLAY MUSIC.

Mike the chicken lived for 18 months without a head, from 1945 to 1947.

A Harley-Davidson MOTORCYCLE WAS designed to look like a giant hamburger.

Chimpanzees, monkeys, dogs, mice, and a guinea pig have all journeyed into space.

One of the largest man-made islands is shaped like a palm tree.

You can buy a **diamond dog collar** for about **$3 million.**

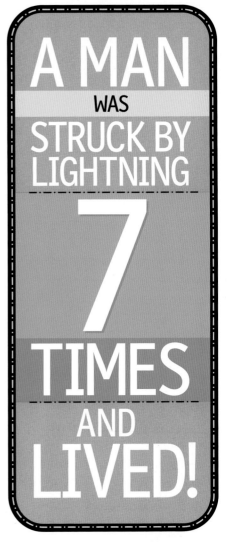

A MAN WAS STRUCK BY LIGHTNING 7 TIMES AND LIVED!

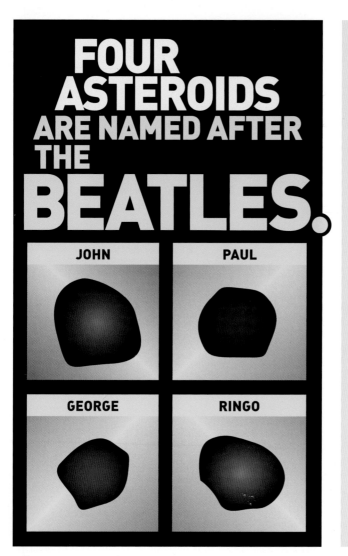

FOUR ASTEROIDS ARE NAMED AFTER THE BEATLES.

JOHN

PAUL

GEORGE

RINGO

If you fell into a black hole, you'd stretch out like s p a g h e t t i.

Crickets detect sound through their knees.

THERE IS CELL PHONE RECEPTION AT THE SUMMIT OF MOUNT EVEREST.

SOME **wild** turkeys **run** UP TO **25** miles (40 km) an hour.

A BAKING COMPANY CREATED A CHOCOLATE CHIP COOKIE THAT WEIGHED AS MUCH AS SEVEN PICKUP TRUCKS.

A COMET is a gigantic ball of dirt and ice.

The **smallest** monkey is about as tall as a **toothbrush.**

A GRIZZLY BEAR CAN RUN AS FAST AS A HORSE.

Astronauts have grown **potatoes** on the **space** shuttle.

A man once rode a bike down the Eiffel Tower's 1,665 steps.

The holes in **Swiss** cheese are called "eyes."

A CANADIAN COMPANY BOTTLES WATER THAT COMES FROM 12,000- TO 15,000- YEAR-OLD ICEBERGS.

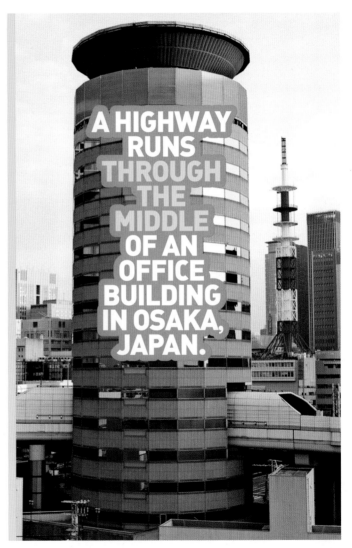

A HIGHWAY RUNS THROUGH THE MIDDLE OF AN OFFICE BUILDING IN OSAKA, JAPAN.

THE WORLD'S MOST EXPENSIVE TREE HOUSE, LOCATED IN THE UNITED KINGDOM, COST £3.7 MILLION TO BUILD.

(about $6.1 million)

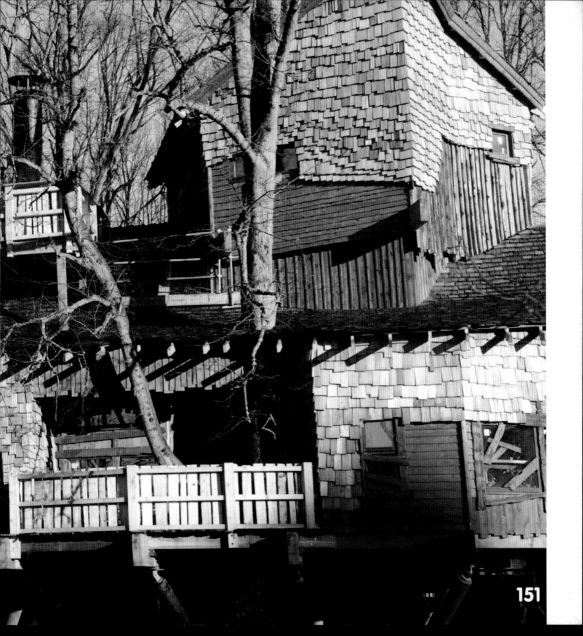

A GREAT WHITE SHARK CAN WEIGH AS MUCH AS 15 GORILLAS.

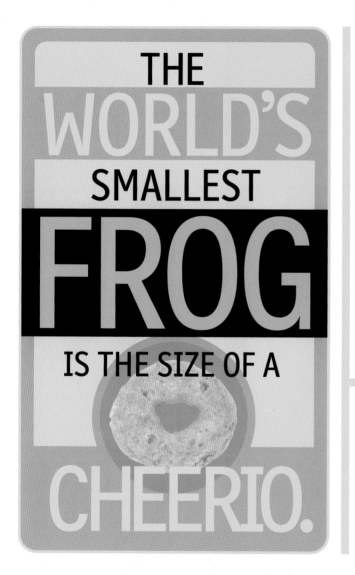

THE **WORLD'S** SMALLEST **FROG** IS THE SIZE OF A **CHEERIO.**

A pizza topped with 24-karat gold sold for more than $4,000.

The world's **termites outweigh** the world's **people.**

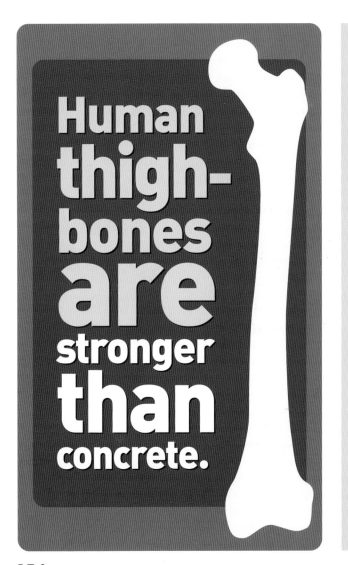

Human thigh-bones are stronger than concrete.

THE PLANET
EARTH
ROTATES

1.5
MILLISECONDS
SLOWER
EVERY
CENTURY.

Snowflakes get smaller as the **TEMPERATURE DROPS.**

A JELLYFISH CAN BE AS SMALL AS A THIMBLE OR AS LARGE AS TWO WASHING MACHINES.

A STACK OF A BILLION DOLLAR BILLS WEIGHS MORE THAN 15 ARMY TANKS.

A **newborn kangaroo** is about as long as a **paper clip.**

Giant anteaters can

A BABY PORCUPINE IS CALLED A PORCUPETTE.

A peanut is not a nut.

THE **FIRST** TELEPHONE ANSWERING **MACHINE** WAS **3** FEET TALL.
(0.9 m)

eat more than 30,000 insects in a day.

There are
31,556,926
seconds
in a year.

THE

BIGGEST
INHABITED
PALACE
ON
EARTH

(IN THE SOUTHEAST ASIAN COUNTRY OF BRUNEI)

HAS

1,788

ROOMS.

A CLOUD CAN WEIGH MORE THAN A MILLION POUNDS.
(453,593 kg)

The Amazon rain forest is home to giant rodents— called capybaras— that are about as tall as German shepherds.

The Chihuahua is the world's smallest dog breed.

Most experts believe that birds are descended from dinosaurs.

20% of the food we eat is used to fuel THE BRAIN.

MARSHMALLOWS WERE ORIGINALLY MADE FROM ROOTS OF A PLANT CALLED THE MARSH-MALLOW.

EVERY DAY IS ABOUT 55 BILLIONTHS OF A SECOND LONGER THAN THE DAY BEFORE IT.

The skin of a golden **poison dart** frog contains enough toxins to kill up to **100** people.

Gorillas **burp** when they're **happy.**

HUMMINGBIRDS are the only birds that can fly **BACKWARD.**

ABOUT ONE-QUARTER OF THE
body's bones are in the feet —that's 52 out of more than 200!

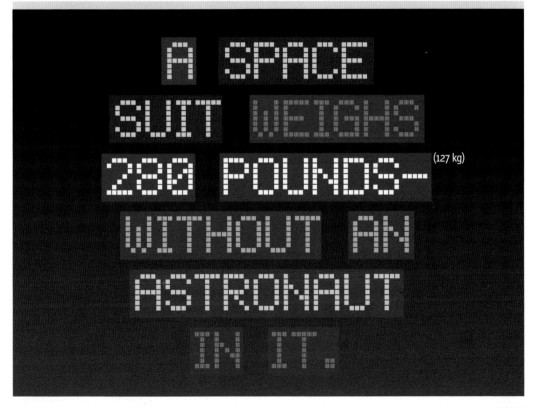

A SPACE SUIT WEIGHS 280 POUNDS— (127 kg) WITHOUT AN ASTRONAUT IN IT.

Elephants sometimes make **purr-like** sounds when content.

Baby
RATTLESNAKES
are born without
RATTLES.

The **Milky Way** is made up of **some 100 billion** stars.

SOME SAND DUNES *BARK.*

You use **72** different muscles every time you talk.

Your body contains about 60,000 miles of blood vessels.

(96,561 km)

Strawberries have more **VITAMIN C** than oranges.

Palm trees
grew at the
North Pole
about 55 million years ago.

A SNAIL
WOULD TAKE ABOUT
220 HOURS
TO CRAWL
ONE MILE
(1.6 km)

NONSTOP.

The
Basenji,
a dog from
Africa,
yodels
instead of
barking.

ON NEPTUNE THE WIND BLOWS UP TO 1,243 MILES (2,000 km) AN HOUR.

"HAPPY BIRTHDAY" WAS THE FIRST SONG TRANSMITTED FROM SPACE TO EARTH.

THE WORLD'S LONGEST
mountain
range
is under the
sea.

An average adult's **skin** **weighs** about **11** **pounds.**

(5 kg)

IF YOU EAT TOO MANY CARROTS, YOUR SKIN CAN TURN ORANGE.

A CROCODILE CAN'T STICK ITS TONGUE OUT.

THE NUMBER OF TIMES **some crickets chirp** each second **can be used to estimate** the **temperature.**

You lose about **NINE POUNDS** (4.1 kg) of skin cells every year.

You can't move your body when you're dreaming.

ARACHIBUTYROPHOBIA IS THE **FEAR** OF GETTING PEANUT BUTTER STUCK TO THE ROOF OF YOUR **MOUTH.**

The
face in the
"Mona Lisa"
has no
eye-
brOws.

You're
almost
a half
inch
taller (1.3 cm)
in the
morning
than
in the
evening.

Astronauts
can't whistle
ON
THE
MOON.

Death Valley, California, is the hottest PLACE IN North America.

Human ears evolved from ancient **FISH GILLS.**

THAT'S WEIRD!

THE LONGEST RECORDED
FLIGHT OF A

ALL OF THE BLOOD IN YOUR BODY TRAVELS THROUGH YOUR HEART ONCE A MINUTE.

IT'S IMPOSSIBLE TO BREATHE AND SWALLOW AT THE SAME TIME.

*CHICKEN IS **13** SECONDS.*

THE OLDEST HUMAN FOOTPRINT EVER FOUND IS 350,000 YEARS OLD.

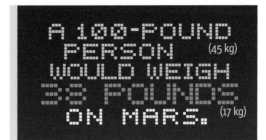

A 100-POUND PERSON (45 kg) WOULD WEIGH 38 POUNDS ON MARS. (17 kg)

Your

hair

grows faster IN WARM WEATHER.

THE MALE KILLER WHALE'S DORSAL (BACK) FIN IS ALMOST SIX FEET (1.8 m) HIGH— THE HEIGHT OF A TALL MAN.

A **LIZARD-LIKE** REPTILE CALLED A TUATARA HAS A **THIRD EYE** ON TOP OF ITS **HEAD.**

191

THE YEAR
2020
is the next time you can see a full moon **on Halloween.**

GHOST BATS are some of the only bats with WHITE FUR.

Sharks have eight senses.

A **coyote** can hear a mouse moving **under a foot of snow.**

Humans have only five.

The **human body** contains enough **iron** to make a two-inch **nail.**

(5.1 cm)

CROCODILES HAVE BEEN AROUND FOR ABOUT

200 MILLION YEARS.

MOUNTAIN LIONS CAN WHISTLE.

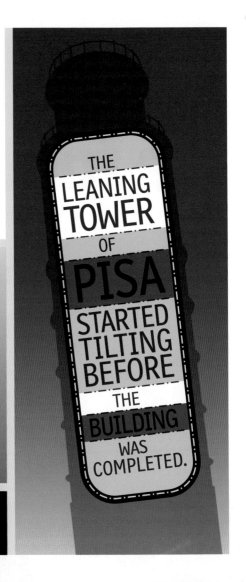

THE LEANING TOWER OF PISA STARTED TILTING BEFORE THE BUILDING WAS COMPLETED.

It's impossible for a person to **sink** in the **Dead Sea.**

Your heart is about the same size as your **fist.**

THE HORNED DINOSAUR *DRACOREX HOGWARTSIA* WAS NAMED AFTER **HOGWARTS,** HARRY POTTER'S SCHOOL.

MORE WATER IS IN THE PACIFIC OCEAN THAN IN ALL OF THE OTHER SEAS AND OCEANS COMBINED.

99%

of people can't
lick their
elbows.

(But 90% of people who read this will try!)

FACTFINDER

Illustrations are indicated by **boldface.**

FACTFINDER

The National Geographic Society is one of the world's largest nonprofit scientific and educational organizations. Founded in 1888 to "increase and diffuse geographic knowledge," the Society works to inspire people to care about the planet. It reaches more than 325 million people worldwide each month through its official journal, NATIONAL GEOGRAPHIC, and other magazines; National Geographic Channel; television documentaries; music; radio; films; books; DVDs; maps; exhibitions; school publishing programs; interactive media; and merchandise. National Geographic has funded more than 9,000 scientific research, conservation and exploration projects and supports an education program combating geographic illiteracy.

For more information, go online.
nationalgeographic.com

Call 1-800-NGS LINE (647-5463) or write to the following address:

NATIONAL GEOGRAPHIC SOCIETY
1145 17th Street NW
Washington, D.C. 20036-4688 U.S.A.

Published by the National Geographic Society
John M. Fahey, Jr., *President and Chief Executive Officer*
Gilbert M. Grosvenor, *Chairman of the Board*
Tim T. Kelly, *President, Global Media Group*
John Q. Griffin, *President, Publishing*
Nina D. Hoffman, *Executive Vice President, President of Book Publishing Group*
Melina Gerosa Bellows, *Executive Vice President of Children's Publishing, Editor in Chief of* NATIONAL GEOGRAPHIC KIDS *magazine*

Prepared by the Book Division
Nancy Laties Feresten, *Vice President, Editor in Chief, Children's Books*
Jonathan Halling, *Design Director, Children's Publishing*
Jennifer Emmett, *Executive Editor, Reference and Solo, Children's Books*
Carl Mehler, *Director of Maps*
R. Gary Colbert, *Production Director*
Jennifer A. Thornton, *Managing Editor*

Staff for This Book
Robin Terry, *Project Editor*
Eva Absher, *Art Direction and Design*
Lori Renda, Jay Sumner, *Illustrations Editors*
Sharon Thompson, Kelsey Turek, *Research*
Grace Hill, *Associate Managing Editor*
Jeff Reynolds, *Marketing Director, Children's Books*
Lewis R. Bassford, *Production Manager*
Susan Borke, *Legal and Business Affairs*

Based on the "Weird But True" department in NATIONAL GEOGRAPHIC KIDS **magazine**
Jonathan Halling, *Design Director*
Robin Terry, *Senior Editor*
Kelley Miller, *Photo Editor*
Sharon Thompson, *Writer-Researcher*
Marilyn Terrell, Mridula Srinivasan, Jeffrey Wandel, *Freelance Researchers*

Manufacturing and Quality Management
Christopher A. Liedel, *Chief Financial Officer*
Phillip L. Schlosser, *Vice President*
Chris Brown, *Technical Director*
Rachel Faulise, *Manufacturing Manager*
Nicole Elliott, *Manufacturing Manager*